僕が見た アフガニスタン

Afghan Blue

久保田弘信 写真集

虹有社

本書に寄せて

私は国連難民高等弁務官として、
その後は日本政府のアフガニスタン復興支援総理特別代表として、
そして現在はJICAの理事長として、
アフガニスタン難民の保護、復興支援、平和構築に取り組んで参りました。
久保田さんの写真は、大変困難な状況に置かれている
アフガニスタンの人たちの日常生活と彼らの表情を色鮮やかに描き出しています。
多くの方がこの写真集を手にとられ、アフガニスタンの人たちの現在、
そして未来に思いをはせていただきたいと思っております。

Having served as the UN High Commissioner for Refugees,
then as the Special Representative of Prime Minister of Japan
on Afghanistan Assistance and currently
as the President of Japan International Cooperation Agency,
I have been working with Afghan people through protecting refugees,
and social and economic reconstruction.
Photographs of Mr. Kubota describe the daily life
and emotion of Afghan people in brilliant color.
I hope that many people will have the chance to ponder over the present
and future of Afghanistan with its people through his artistic work.

緒方 貞子
Sadako Ogata

ナッサルバール難民キャンプ。
Refugee camp at Nasir Bagh.

上：カブールからマザリシャリフへ向かう峠。
4000メートル級の峠を越えるとき、
山羊の群れを放牧させているシーンに出会った。
右：マザリシャリフ郊外。
見渡す限りの土漠地帯でたった一人でロバにのる少女。

Above: At the elevation of 4,000 meter and above, running into a herd of goats on a mountain pass from Kabul to Mazar-e-Sharif.
Right: Suburban Mazar-e-Sharif. Solitary donkey rider on the plateau of endless desert.

壊れた戦車で遊ぶ子どもたち。カンダハル。
Children playing on a broken tank, Kandahar.

糸を紡ぐ子ども。
ラティファバード難民キャンプ。
Child with spindle.
Latifabad refugee camp.

アフガニスタンにて

Living in Afghanistan

カブール。
Kabul.

上:カブールの街並み。下:内戦で破壊された街。カブール。
Above: Streets of Kabul. Bottom: War-torn city, Kabul.

上:カンダハル警察署。下:モスク。カンダハル。
Above: Kandahar Police Station. Bottom: Mosque, Kandahar.

香辛料を売る子ども。ジャララバード。
Child selling spices, Jalalabad.

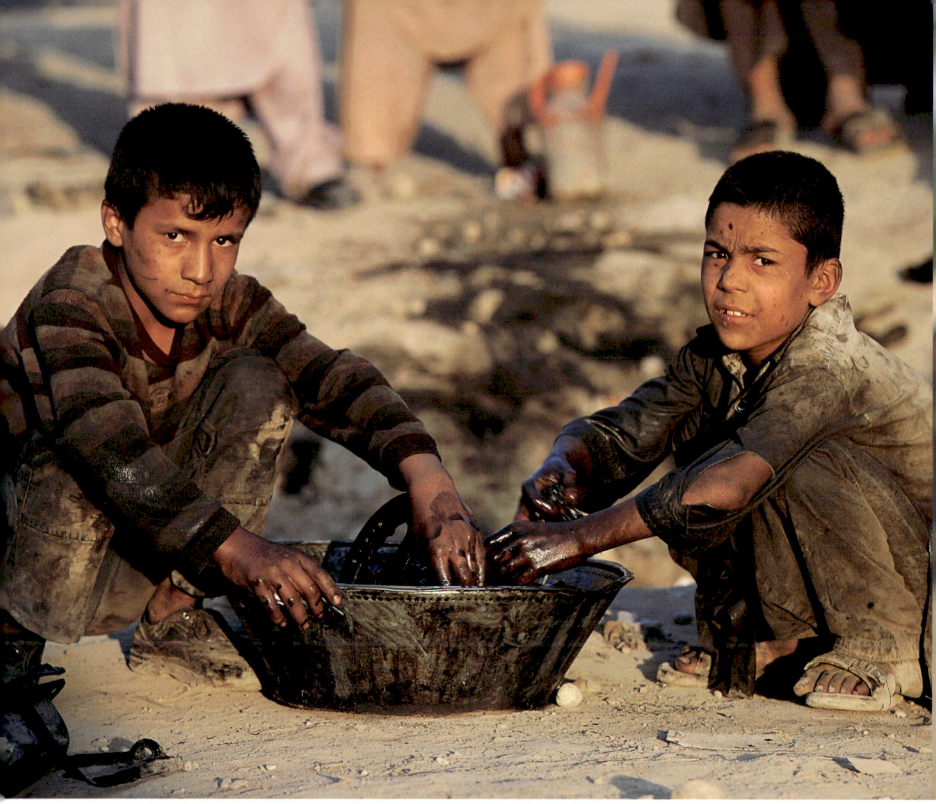
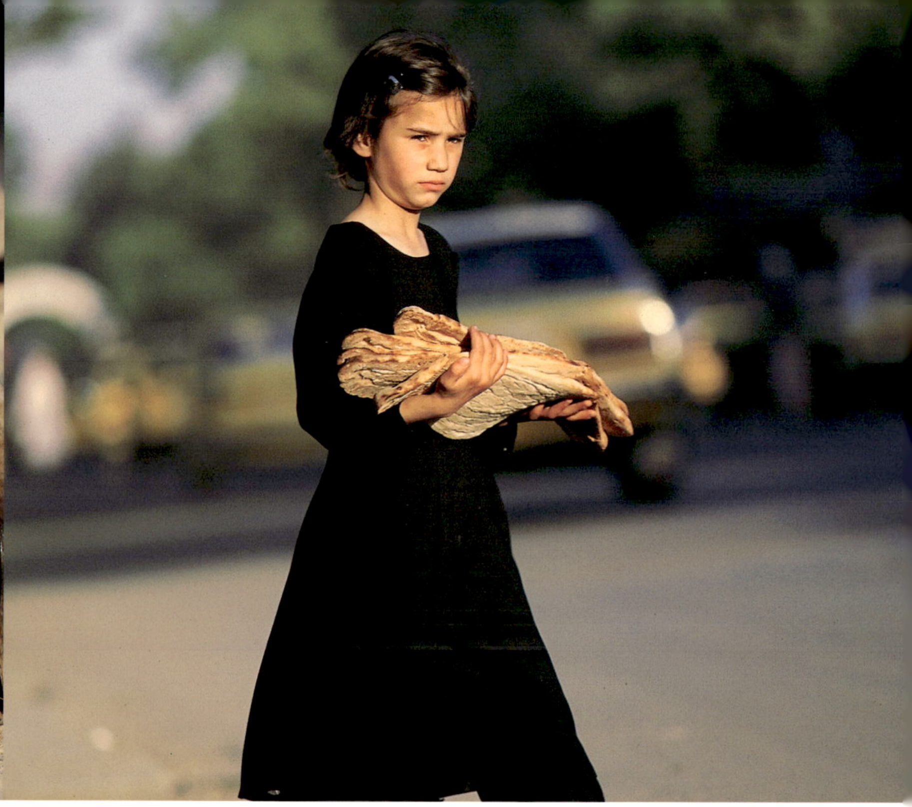
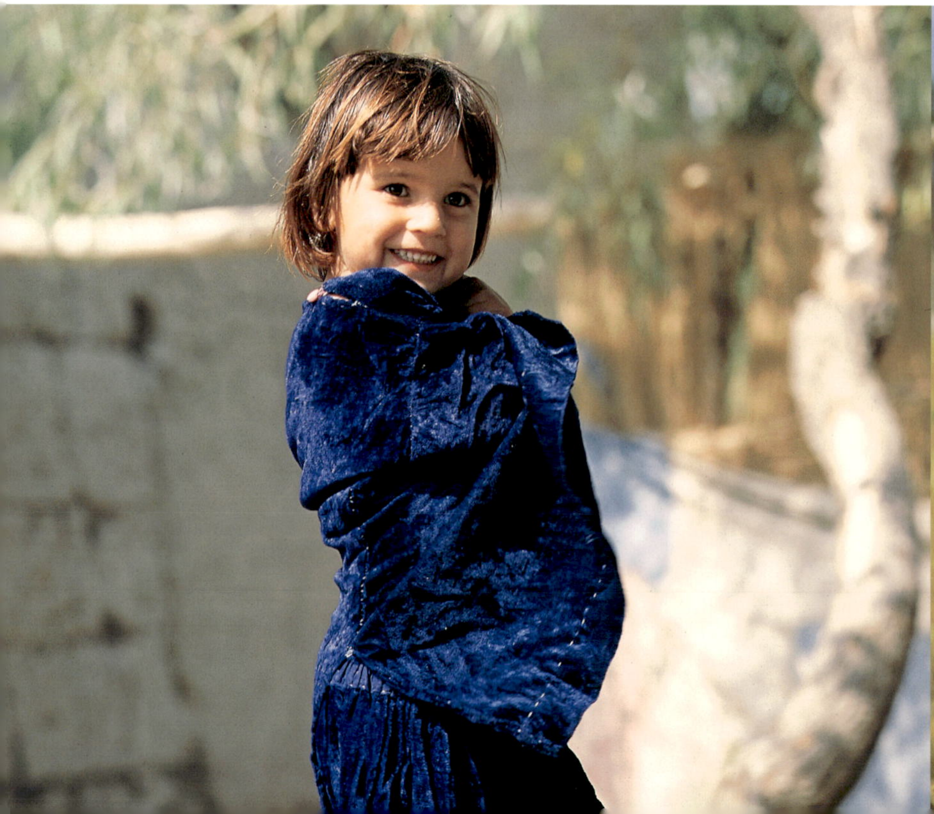
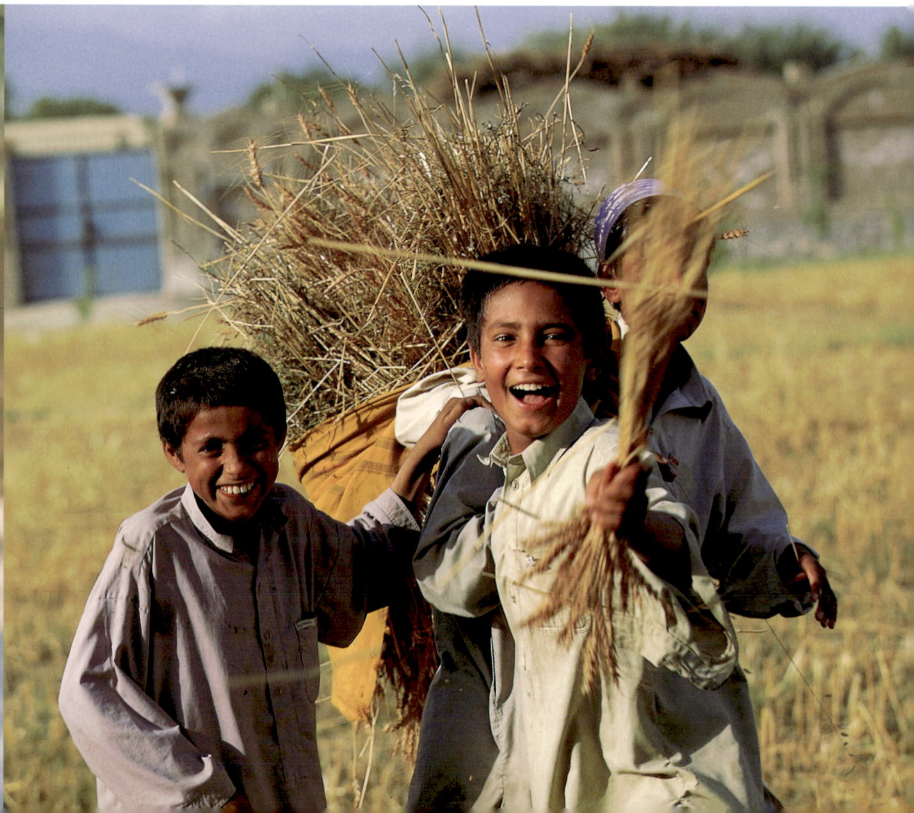

アフガニスタンの子どもたち。
マザリシャリフ、カブール、
ジャララバードにて。

Children in Afghanistan.
Mazar-e-Sharif, Kabul,
Jalalabad.

オアシスのような場所に
毎日村人が水を汲みにくる。
マザリシャリフ郊外。

Villagers make a daily trip to
this oasis-like area for water.
Mazar-e-Sharif suburb.

上、下：収穫を喜ぶ人々。マザリシャリフ郊外。
Above and Bottom: Farmers celebrating harvest, Mazar-e-Sharif suburbs.

マザリシャリフ郊外。
Suburban Mazar-e-Sharif.

ジャララバード郊外の学校。
木陰でひと休みする学生達。

Suburban Jalalabad school.
Students relaxing away from the sun.

車が通れる道はなく、
ラクダやロバが活躍する。

Camels and donkeys replace
automobiles on roads like this.

地雷について勉強する子どもたち。
ジャララバード。

Children learning about
land mine, Jalalabad.

学校へ行く子どもたち。アチン（ジャララバード郊外）。Children commuting to school, Achin. Jalalabad suburbs.

上：地雷について勉強する子どもたち。ジャララバード郊外。
下：学校。マザリシャリフ。

Above: Children learning about land mine, Jalalabad suburbs.
Bottom: School in Mazar-e-Sharif.

27

原野の子どもたち。
マザリシャリフ郊外。

Children out in the field,
Suburban Mazar-e-Sharif.

左：収穫物を運ぶ。マザリシャリフ郊外。
右：アフガニスタンの伝統音楽を披露してくれた。ダライエヌール。

Left: Man with harvest on his shoulder, Mazar-e-Sharif Surburbs.
Right: Playing Afghanistan's traditional music. Dara-e-Noor.

空爆で破壊された家の前に
佇む子どもたち。カンダハル。
Standing besides a bombed house, Kandahar.

カンダハル。
Kandahar.

戦争で亡くなった人たちの墓。カンダハル。
Victims of war, Kandahar.

左：地雷除去。ジャララバード郊外。右：誤爆を受けた村ソルフロッド（ジャララバード郊外）。
Left: Demining, Jalalabad suburbs. Right: Village bombed by mistake, Jalalabad suburb.

サマリー。女の子は少女と母親の両方の顔を持っていた。
Samari. Child with a face of both woman and girl.

ジャロザイ難民キャンプ。
Jailozai refugee camp.

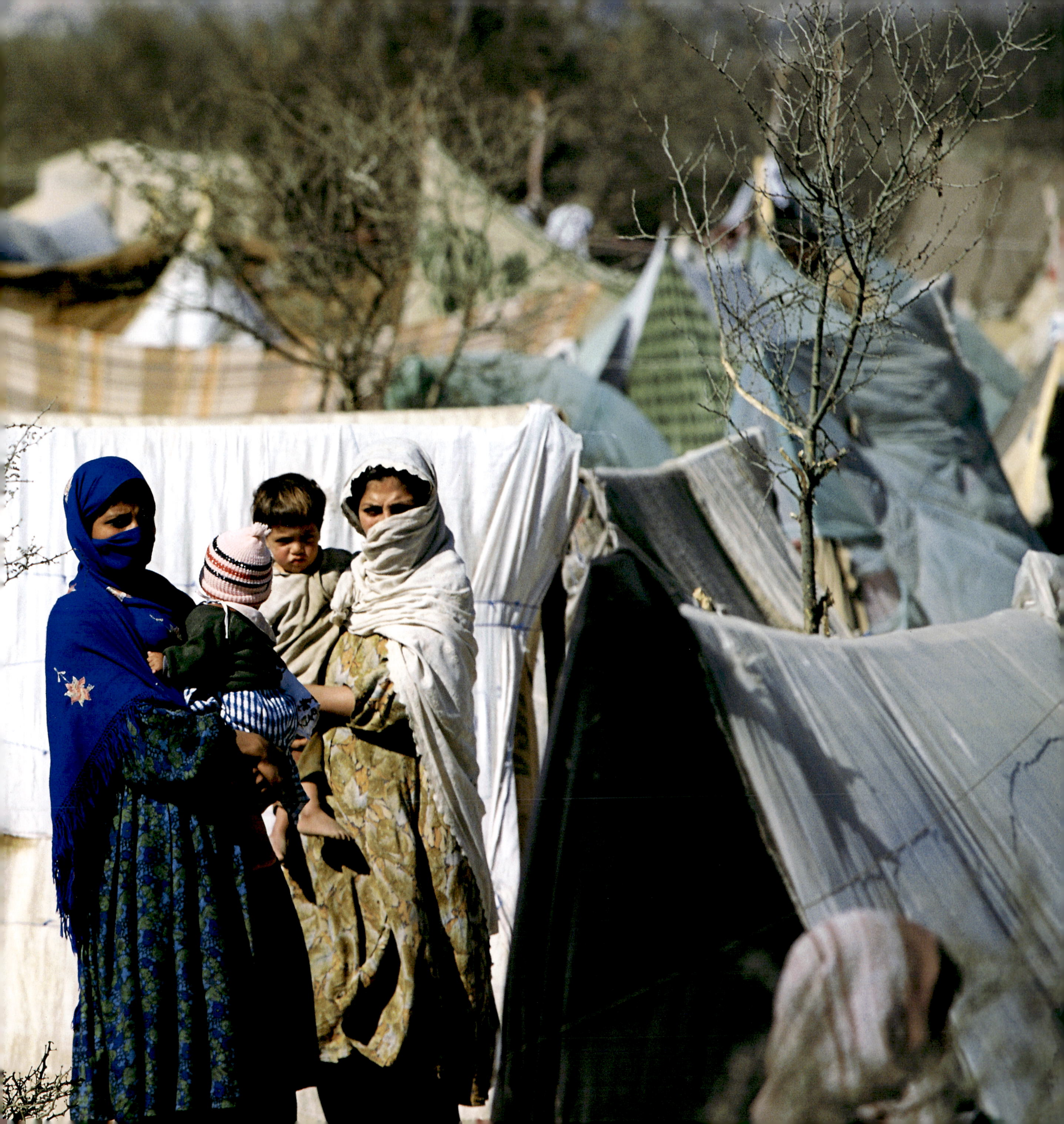

パキスタンの難民キャンプに入れない人たちの為に国境沿いに作られたウエイティングエリア。
境界を作るための有刺鉄線が厳しさを物語る。

Waiting area along the border for refugees who were refused admission into camps in Pakistan.
Barbed wire creating the boundaries reveals the harsh truth.

サリプル国内避難民キャンプ。
Sar-epol IDP Camp.

パンを運ぶ少女。
シャムシャトゥー。
Shamshatoo.
A girl carrying breads.

モハメッドヘイル難民キャンプ。
難民キャンプでの子どもたちの
一番の仕事は水くみだ。

Mohammad Kheil refugee camp. Delivering water is always a No.1 duty for children at the camp.

井戸の回りに集まった子どもたち。
ナッサルバール難民キャンプ。

Children surrounding the well.
Nasir Bagh refugee camp.

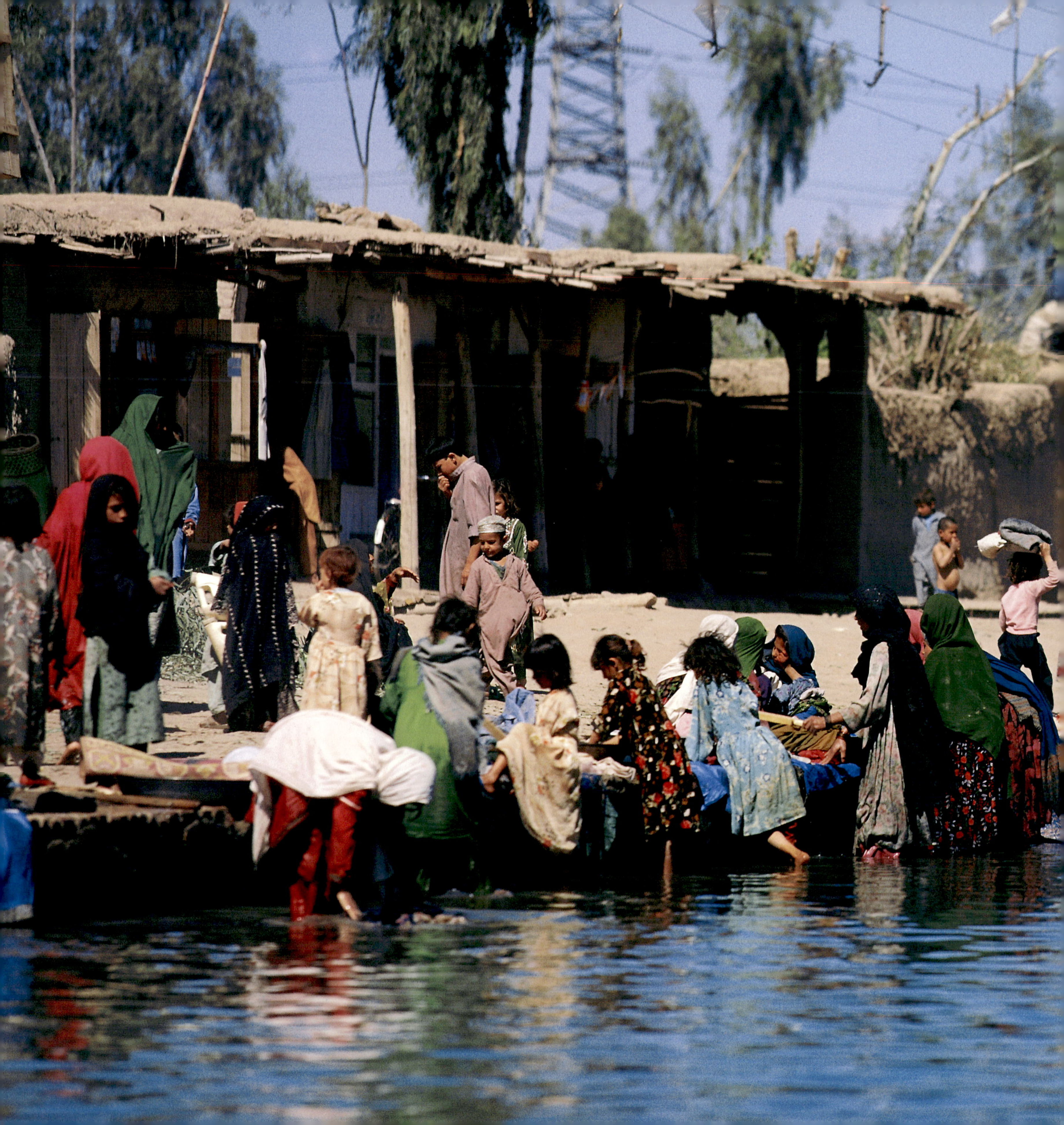

難民キャンプと外の世界の
国境のような川。
ナッサルバール難民キャンプ。

The river separates the camp
from "outside".
Nasir Bagh refugee camp.

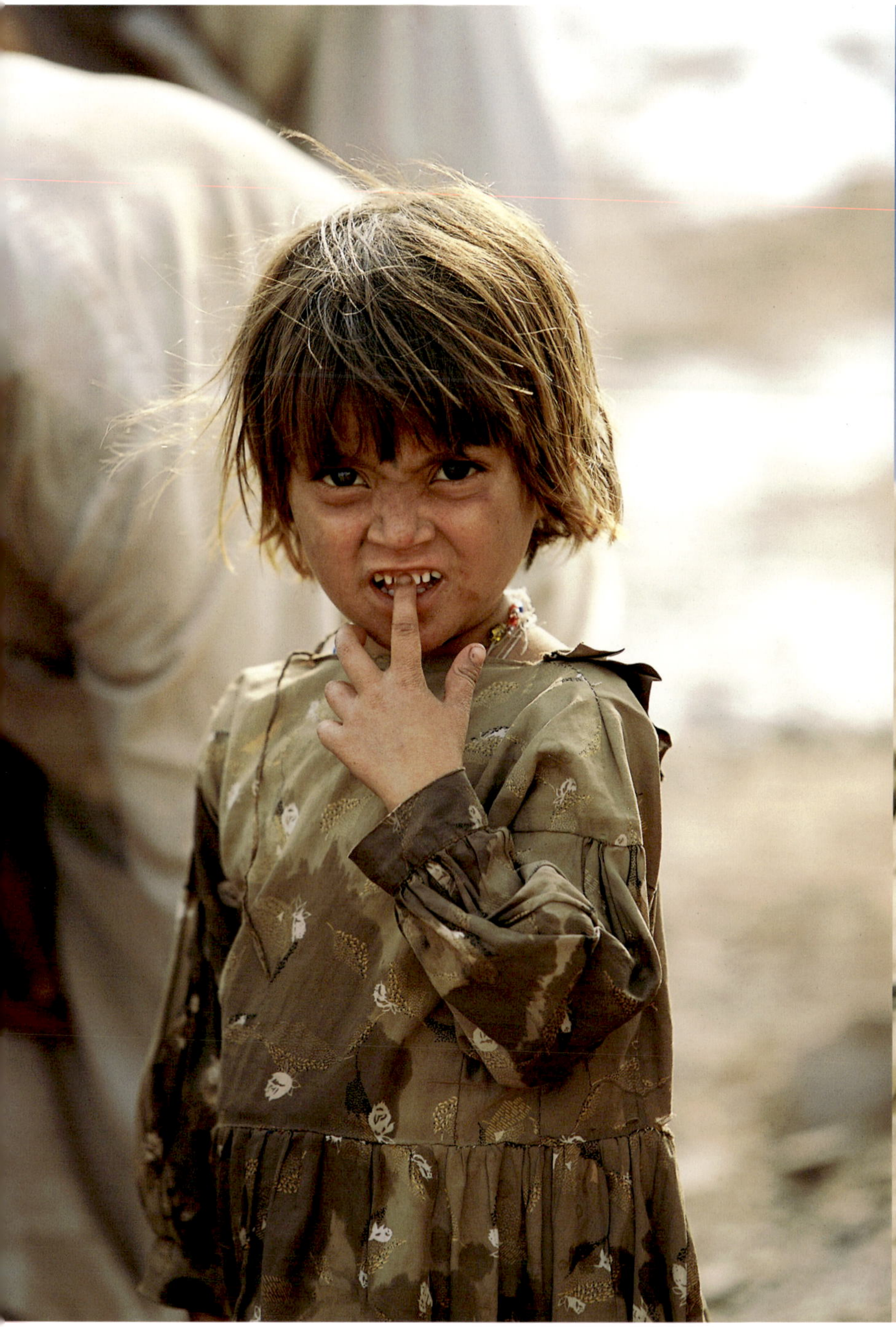
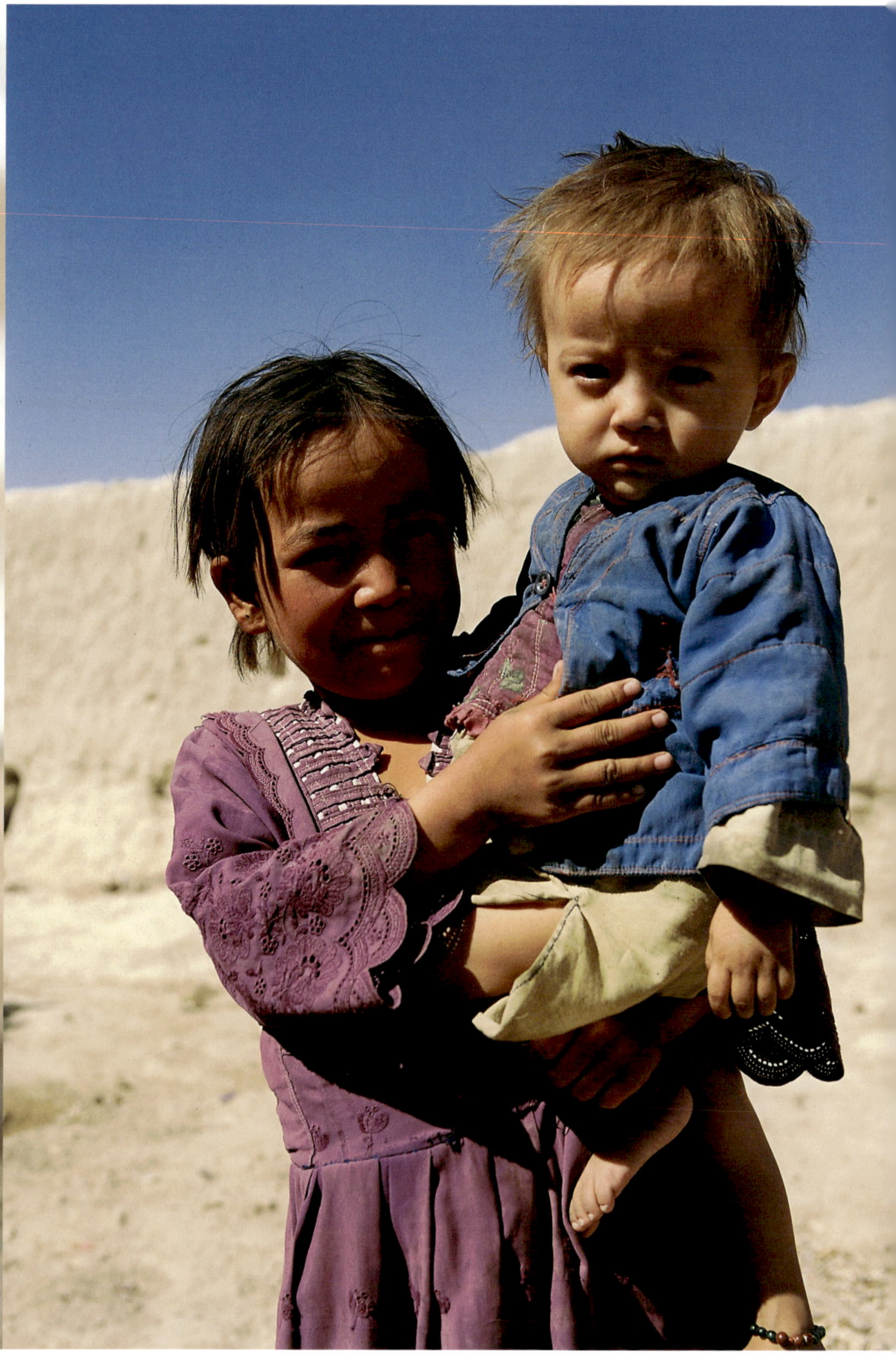

左から、ジャロザイ、サマリー、ナッサルバール、モハメッドヘイル。
From the left, Jailozai, Samari, Nasir Bagh, Mohammad Kheil.

モハメッドヘイル。
Mohammad Kheil.

ナッサルバール。
Nasir Bagh.

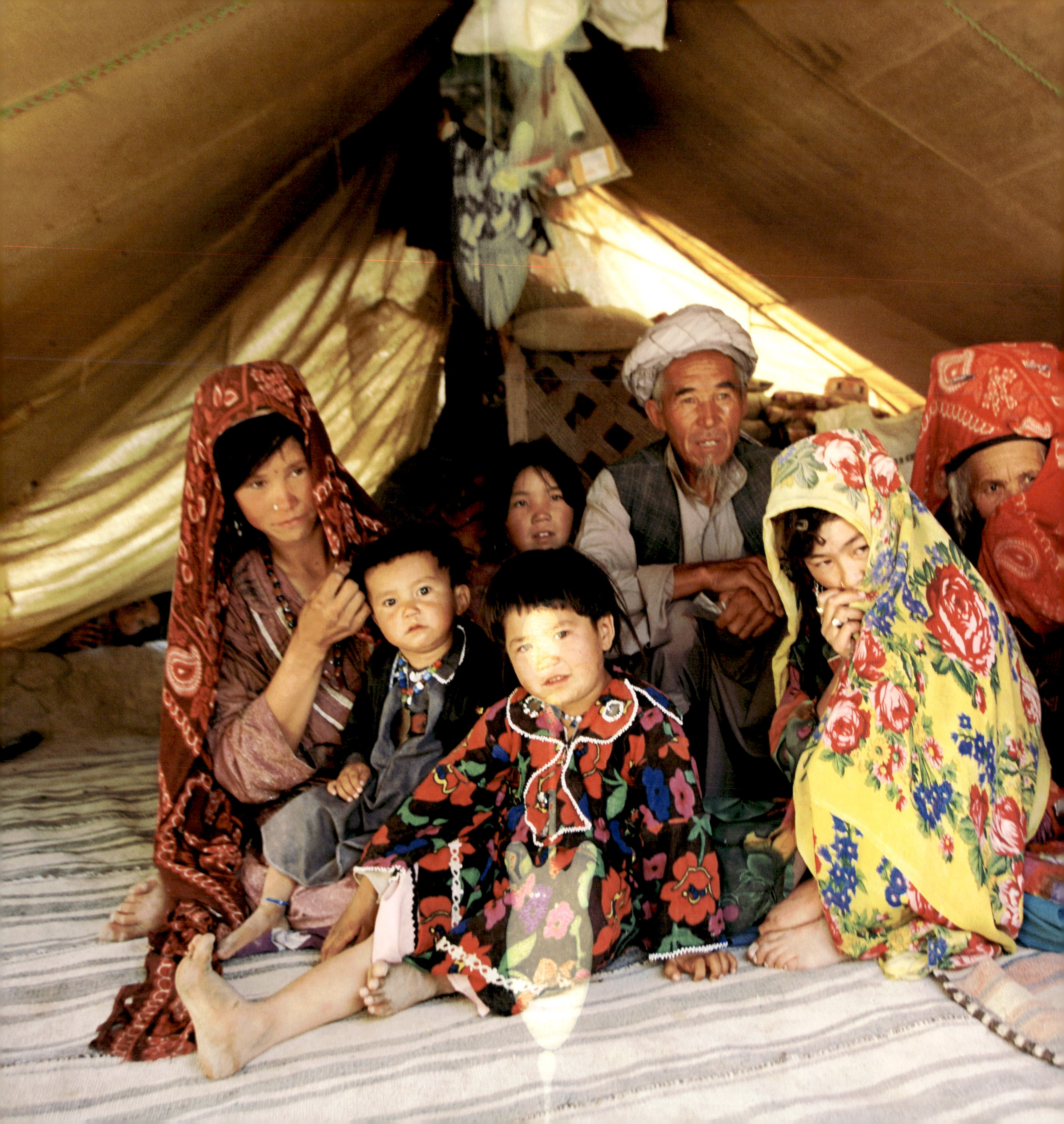

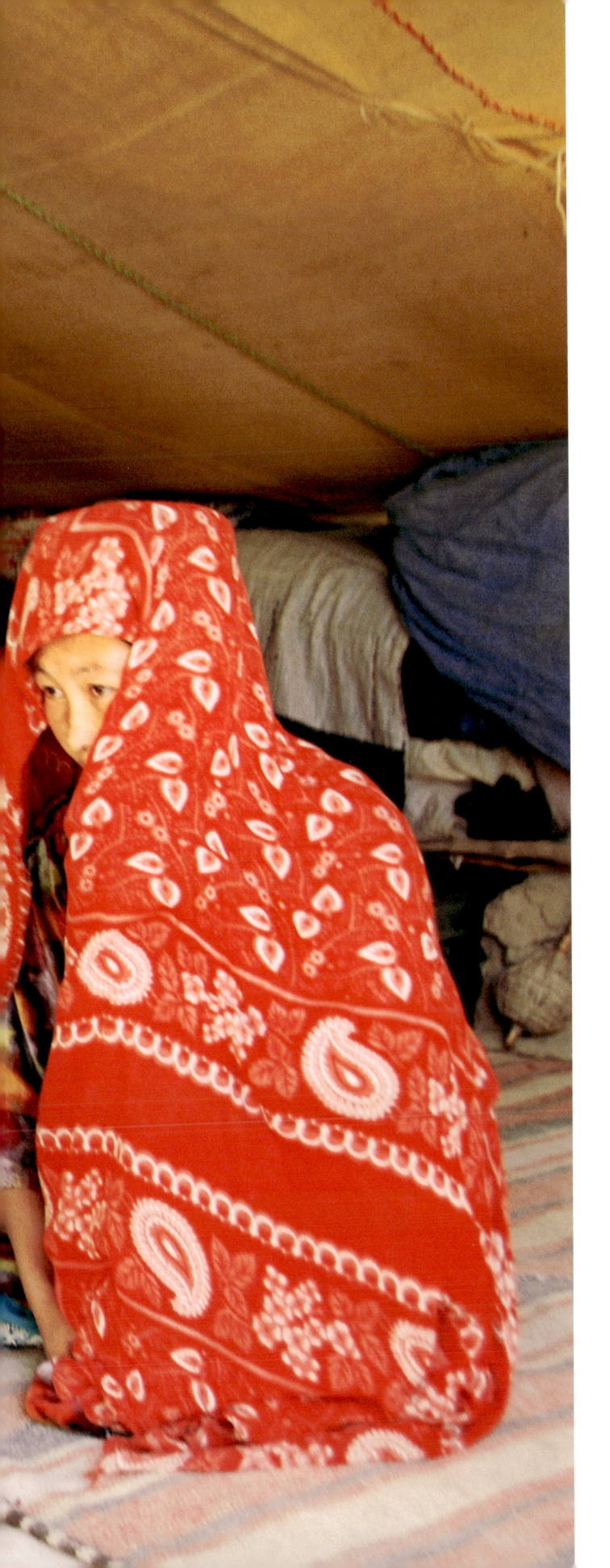

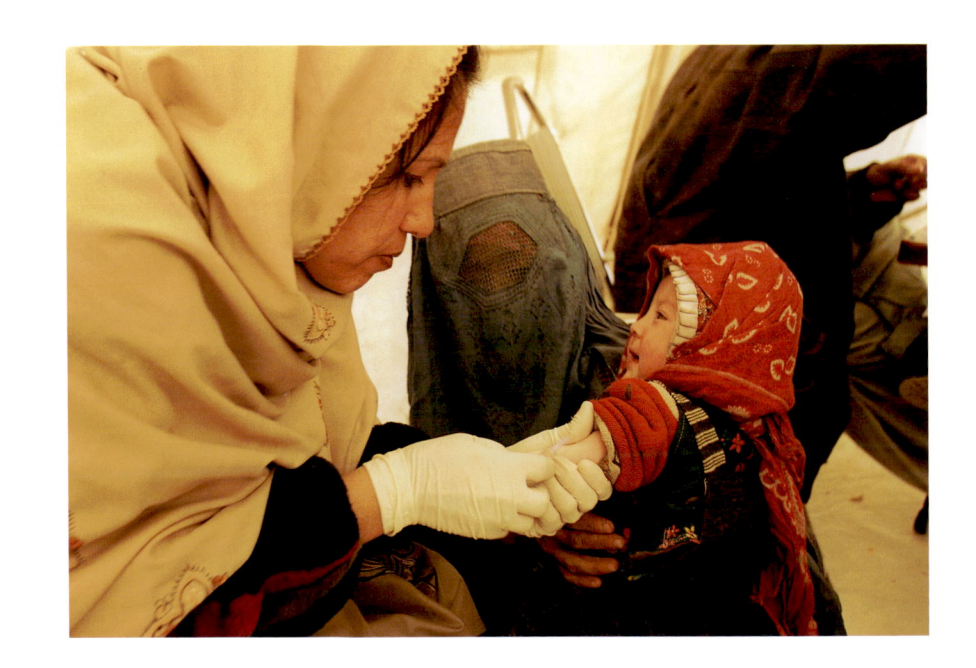

難民キャンプに着いた子どもたちは、
一番に予防接種を受ける。
ラティファバード。
Children were vaccinated upon
arrival to the camp.
Latifabad.

サマリー難民キャンプ。
Samari refugee camp.

難民キャンプに入れない人々が、
国境沿いのウエイティングエリアに
集められた。環境はとても
過酷なものだった。

People who were not allowed to enter the refugee camp gathered along the border. Circumstance was harsh.

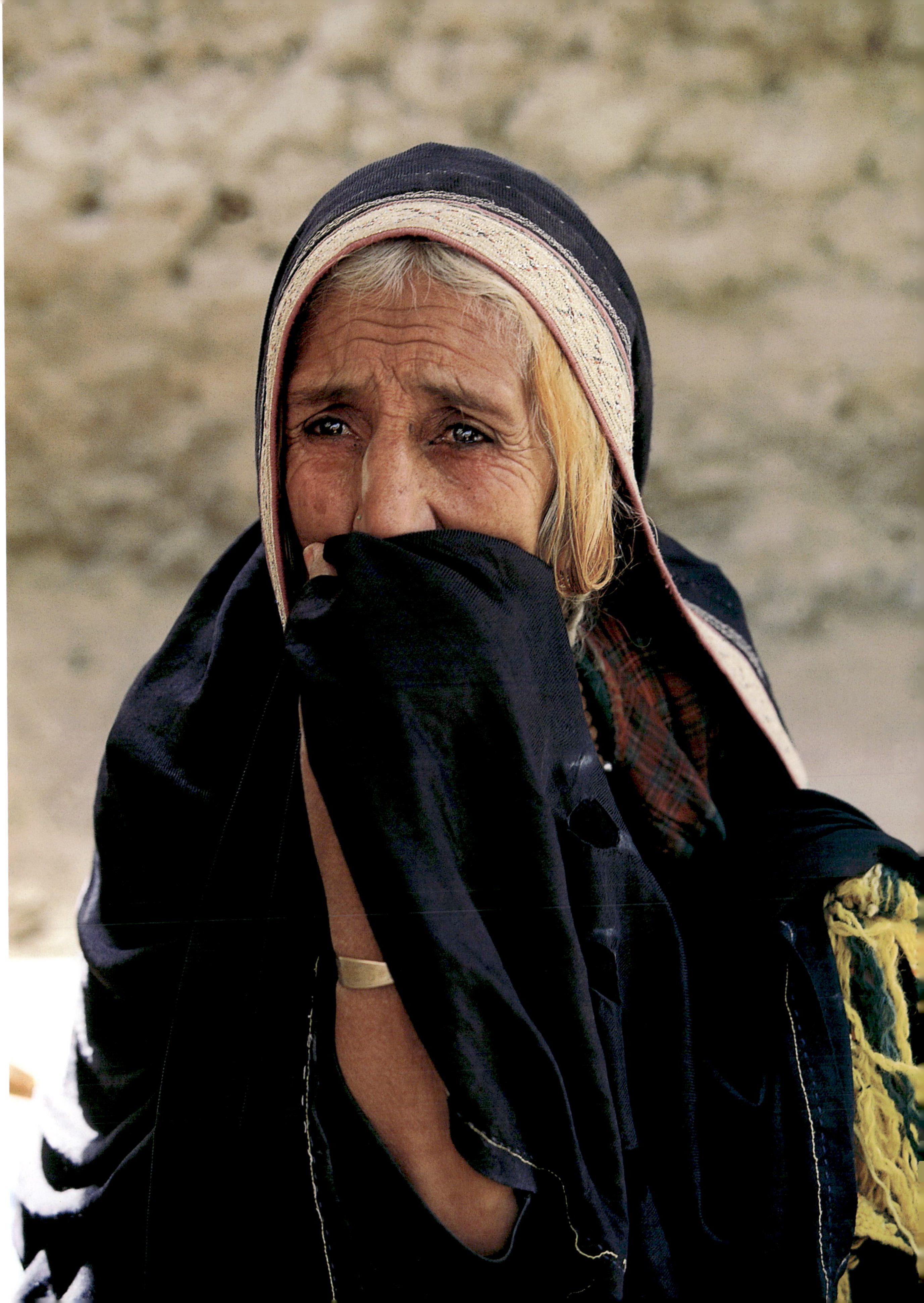

少数民族のウズベク人は、
大多数のパシュトゥン人がいる
モハメッドヘイル難民キャンプに
入ることができなかった。
そのため、国連のサポートを受けられない
サマリー難民キャンプにやってきた。

It was impossible for Uzbek refugees
to enter the camp in Mohammad Kheil
where Pashtun was a majority.
Therefore they went to Samari camp,
which was not supported by UN.

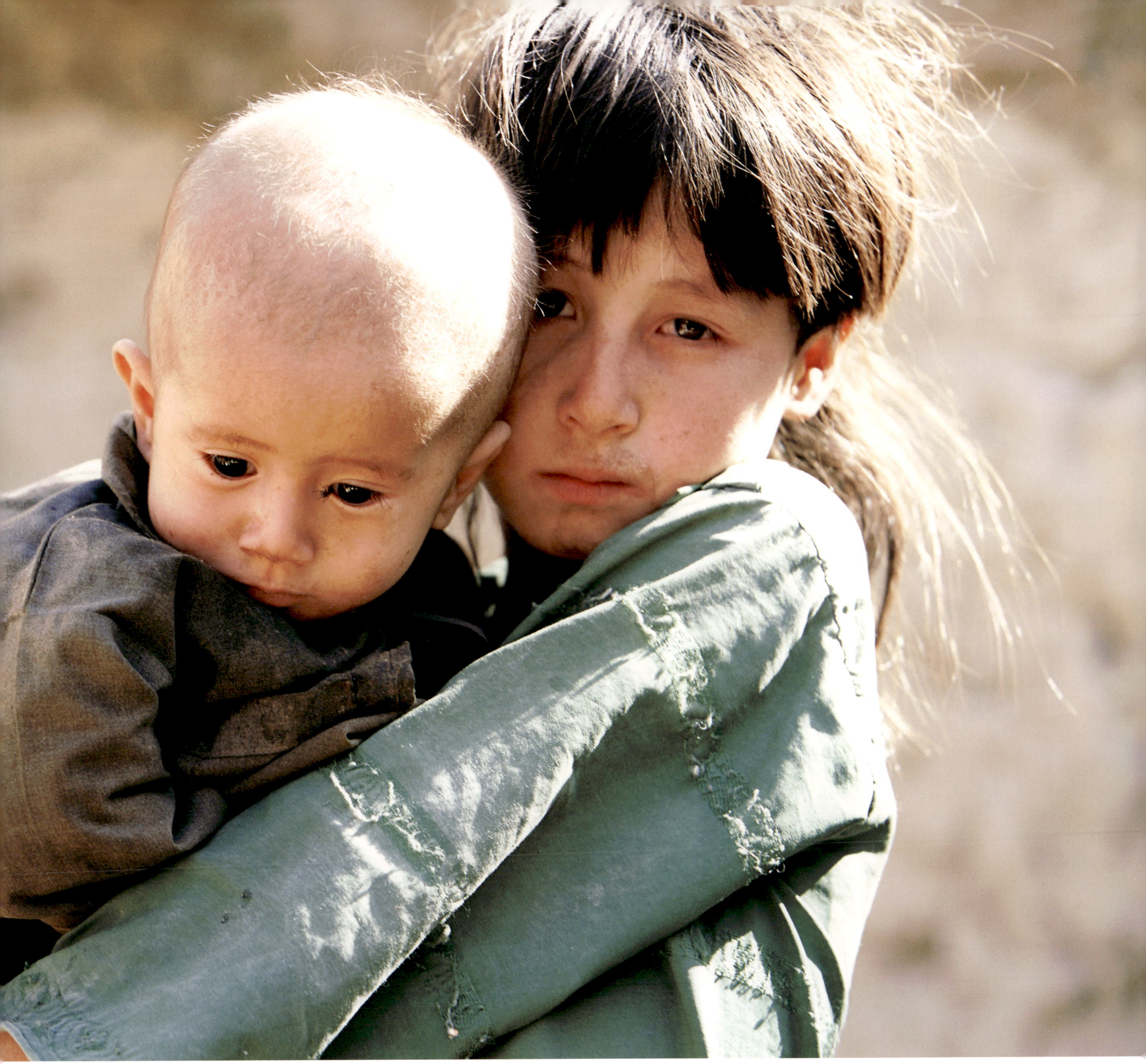

サマリー難民キャンプ。
Samari refugee camp.

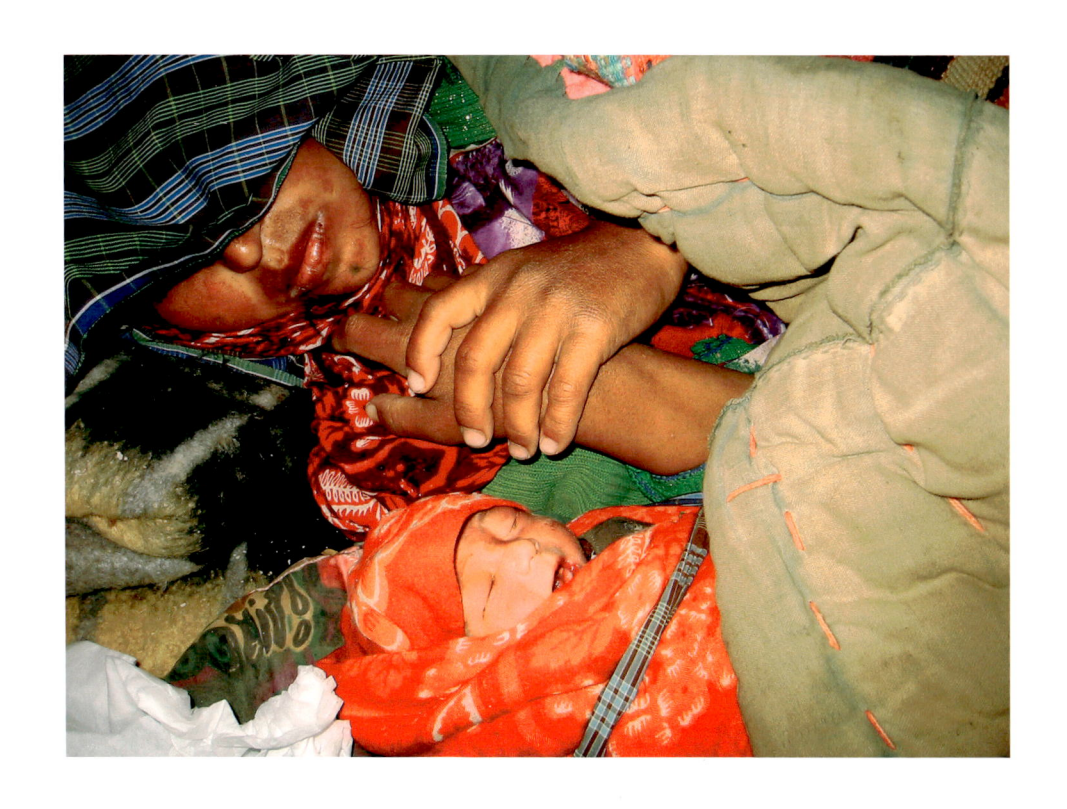

難民キャンプで新たな命が生まれた。
夜は零下になる過酷な環境のなか、
幼い命はたった20日でその火を消してしまった。

Frail new life at the camp
did not reach 20 days old under
cruel sub-zero nights.

未来への祈り

Prayer for the future

クリケットで遊ぶ子どもたち。
ナッサルバール難民キャンプ。
Children playing cricket.
Nasir Bagh refugee camp.

ナッサルバール難民キャンプの学校。
テントが校舎代わりだったが、
新しい校舎が完成して喜ぶ子どもたち。
School at Nasir Bagh refugee camp.
Children enjoying the new school
building which replaced old tents.